How to Talk

Word-For-Word Scripts For The Most
Important Make Or Break Moments From
Meeting A Man To Marriage

BY

MATTHEW COAST

Table of Contents

What Other Women Are Saying

I am now in a happy long term healthy relationship thanks to Matt. I spent so much time dating focusing on my outside personality that I failed to connect on a real level.

Being honest and vulnerable opened up a whole new world following Matt's advice as to how and when to do that was key as well."

Meghan

"Thank you so much. **Your product is absolutely wonderful.** Thank you. I am glad there is someone out there like you for all us single women!"

Rebecca

"**Your program changed my life.** I thank Matthew so much. His advice and techniques are invaluable."

Kim

"**I can vouch that your advice really works!** I met a wonderful man after I started treating myself as valuable enough and realized what I want in a relationship.

I bought both of your programs and studied them carefully and it made me see things differently.

Not long after that, **I met my Mr. Right**! Keep up the good work Matt and ladies, you CAN listen to him!"

Petro

"I just wanted to say thank you!!!!

I stumbled upon you Mr. Coast and your wisdom has touched my conscience and subconscious. I've learned so much and so much has smacked me right in the face. I used to call myself "not girlfriend material" and didn't think I could have a relationship last longer than 8 mo.

But the universe and yourself have thrown on my lap all the tools I need to realize **I AM a woman a quality man wants to be with**.

I am now in the first stages of what could potentially become a good healthy relationship with a good healthy man. And I want to thank you for what you are doing!!;-)"

Mariah

"I'm glad that you have opened up my eyes in terms of how us women should behave in order to get what we want. **This is a must do thing for any woman who would love to be treated like a queen**.. Thanks!!!"

Nozi

"**The program is absolutely amazing**. I don't have to play games or pretend I'm someone I'm not. This guy likes me for who I am and truly accepts me."

Christina

PART 1

Meet Him and Get Him Hooked

Arguably, the most important time in a relationship is the very beginning.

When a man first meets you, he determines whether or not you're relationship material within the very first few minutes.

Surveys were conducted where they asked men what determined whether they wanted to marry a woman or not.

What most men said was that it was the personality of the woman that made them decide that she was the right man for them.

It was what she said and how she communicated with him at the very beginning.

If you say the wrong things to a man, it can stop him cold. It can make him feel like you're the wrong person for him.

It can make him feel like you would fight all the time and not match well together for a long-term relationship.

However, if you communicate and say the right things, it can get him excited about you.

It can make him feel like you're exactly who he's been looking for. It can make him feel like you're the type of woman that he would want to spend the rest of his life with.

And whatever a man determines at the beginning of meeting you, it's incredibly difficult to change his mind after that.

So what do you want to communicate when you first meet a man?

The number 1 most attractive trait that men find in women is **confidence**.

And it's easy to be confident when you know exactly what you're going to say.

That's why it's so important that you have these scripts!

You also want to convey that you're fun and playful.

When you're fun and playful, you'll pull a man out of his thoughts and into his heart.

This is where a man needs to be in order to eventually fall in love with you. He needs to have YOU pull him into his heart.

Men are fascinated by the emotions of women. You may not realize how powerful your emotions are when it comes to men but they can be incredibly attractive if you use them right.

A lot of people talk about having a bit of mystery to you to attract a man.

I have some news for you...

Women are completely mysterious to most men.

Your emotions, your decisions, the way you think and act are a complete mystery to a guy.

If you want to keep that mystery up, stay in your feminine. Connect to your emotions and express them in an attractive way.

That will give you an amazing power over the men you meet.

This first section is all about how to communicate with a man when you first meet him in a way that will make him see you as someone he could potentially be with in a long-term committed relationship.

Commitment
Connection

Get Him to Approach You

Let me tell you a little known secret about men…

Have you ever been so afraid of something that the thought of it put you in paralysis?

Men have a biological response that can make them feel and react this way around one very specific action…

I've spent a good portion of my life facing my fears and challenging my limits.

I skydived dozens of times. I successfully completed what has been known as the most difficult military training in the world.

I've backpacked through dangerous third world countries for months by myself without knowing the language. I've spoken in front of audiences of over 2000 people.

Yet there's one thing that, if I'm about to do it, it grips my body in stress and anxiety almost to the point of paralysis…

And believe it or not, that one thing is this:

Approaching women…

It's true. Approaching women freaks me out, every time.

In fact, any man who doesn't spend a ton of time approaching women feels like this.

In the men's dating community, they call this "approach anxiety." And all men have it from one degree to another.

As far as psychologists can tell, approach anxiety is a male biological function that warns them of the dangers of being rejected by their peers. And it is POWERFUL.

In fact, the more attractive he thinks you are, the more difficult this is for him.

When I first came back from Iraq, I decided that I was going to do whatever it takes to really figure out my dating life.

I started by going out four nights a week, hoping to meet some women.

Guess how many I met... ZERO. I didn't meet ANY (sad, I know).

If you go out and you don't meet anyone, you're just wasting your time. And that's what I was doing...

As soon as I'd see a woman I thought I might want to talk to, I'd start heading straight for her...

About halfway there, approach anxiety would overcome my body with indecision, kind of like a deer staring into headlights, unable to move.

And when I did manage to resist it, I would get over to the woman and what came out of my mouth... well the best way to describe it would be some type of incoherent muttering that I can

only assume would make the women I attempted to talk to think I was either stupid or crazy.

Talk about a humbling experience!

I went home every night in shame and embarrassment.

I thought to myself, "I'm this big, bad military soldier... I shoot guns, jump out of airplanes and blow things up for a living. Yet the thought of approaching a woman half my size... it cripples me!"

There's a myth out there that the men who approach without invitation are somehow better men or higher quality men than those who don't...

Yet after working in the men's dating industry for years, I discovered something very important...

Men Who Approach You Without Invitation Aren't the Highest Quality Men, They're Just the Most Aggressive Ones

Some of these guys are great guys... some of them are sleazy.

But screening men based whether they'll approach without invitation or not doesn't get you the highest quality men, it just gets you the most aggressive ones.

There was a study done where researchers went out to bars and studied the behavior patterns of men who approached women.

What they found is that there's a small, handful of men who approach women all the time.

There's an even smaller group of men who will approach a woman if she seems really interesting to him.

But the overwhelming majority of men (over 85%) will ONLY approach a woman IF she gives him some type of indication that she wants him to approach her.

Guys who approach a lot know that the more often they approach, the more often they get laid.

For most guys though, approaching a woman they don't know is pretty risky.

They have to somehow get close to her, start up a conversation, be interesting to her and hopefully don't get attacked, ridiculed or forced to do the walk of shame back to where they approached from.

And by the way, getting attacked, ridiculed and forced to do the walk of shame is what usually happens to most men who approach...

So if a guy (who isn't super aggressive) thinks this might happen, he may just avoid approaching altogether to save himself the embarrassment.

My point is that if you want a great guy to approach you, you need to make it easy for him to approach you.

Otherwise, you'll only get approached by the most aggressive guys, not the highest quality ones.

Invite a Man Over with Eye Contact and a Smile.

Here are some other things you can do to make yourself approachable when you're out...

Avoid the Large Group Huddle

Have you ever tried to approach a group of people, hoping to talk to one of the women in it while avoiding to anger or piss off the rest of the group?

No?

Well, it can be pretty difficult.

The way to make this easier for a guy is to open your body language outward from the group.

Stay on the outside edge of the group and slightly face your body away from it.

This gives men an indication that you're open to talk to and they don't have to win over your entire group with magic tricks and jokes just to talk to you.

Be Nice to Anyone Who Approaches You

For everything good and just in this world, please be nice to men who come over and approach you.

Not only does this make others who want to approach you feel like they can, it also will help out all other women in the future who want to be approached by men.

Now, sometimes he may need a little bit more than this. If this is the situation with you, you may want to...

Wave Him Over

I actually first had this done to me at a bar in Boulder, Colorado. A woman waved me over to come talk to her and, at first, I was in a bit of disbelief.

But then she started patting the seat next to her and reality set in that she REALLY did want me to come over and talk to her.

I have to admit that I felt like the coolest guy in the bar walking over to talk with her.

It takes a little bit of risk on your part but the worst thing that could probably happen is that he just simply doesn't come over.

The best thing that could happen is that you'd start a conversation with an awesome guy who could end up being Mr. Right.

And for most guys, this is incredibly attractive.

Start a Conversation With Him

Do men like being approached by women?

Unfortunately, the answer is as simple as Yes or No.

Some men like it and some men don't. Some men will be relieved by it and even attracted to it and some men will be turned off by it.

But it's the same with women…

Some women think it's harassment to get approached by a man she doesn't know.

And believe me, I've met quite a few of these women.

But if I never approached them, I would have never found out. And most of the women I've approached in my life were very kind and sweet to me.

And most of the men that you'll meet out there will be very kind and sweet to you if you decide to start up a conversation with them.

But there's also an attractive way to approach a man and an unattractive way to approach him.

If you see a guy you think you might like and he's not coming over to talk to you, your only choice to meet him might be to go over

Commitment Connection

and start up a conversation if you don't want the opportunity to pass you by.

I'm going to give you a few attractive ways to approach a guy...

Here's the first:

Ask him for help with something...

Men love to help women. They want to be your hero. They want to be your knight in shining armor.

And when you ask him for help, it releases that hero part of a man that makes him want to come over and save the day for you.

it doesn't have to be with something big...

You can simply ask him to help you decide what drink to get:

"Hey, can you help me? What's a good drink here?"

You can ask him to help you and a friend settling a debate:

"Hey, my friend and I are trying to settle something... Who's more fun blondes or brunettes?"

You can ask him to help you understand something about men (try to make this fun and not anti-male or it will backfire):

"Hey, can you help me figure something out... why don't men like to ask for directions?"

Or this one...

14

"Maybe you can help me with this... do you think that man who grow up with sisters understand women better?"

Here's a flirty one that you have to do with a straight face then crack a smile at the end of it...

"Hey, I'm conducting a poll and of the most attractive men here... do you like my hair better up or down?"

Ask a man for help with something and he'll come to your rescue.

This can be a great conversation starter and will immediately make him feel like a man around you, which is very attractive.

The second technique is something that can be used anywhere that there's a chair...

All you have to do is look for an open seat next to him and say...

"Is someone sitting here?"

And then follow it up with a...

"Hi, what's your name?"

This is simple, straight-forward and can be really attractive to a guy, especially if he's caught off guard by it.

The third technique I call...

Invite Him to Talk Then Walk.

This can be EXTREMELY attractive to a guy, if done right.

This is a way that you can approach him without risking rejection AND send all the right signals.

Here's how it works...

Walk up to him, look him in the eyes, smile and say this...

"Hey, I'd love it if you'd come over and talk to me."

Then walk away and go sit somewhere.

To a masculine guy, this sends the right message. And if he's attracted to you and single, you better believe he'll come over and talk to you.

Here's the deal... You can sit around and hope that a man will approach you.

If you do and he doesn't pick up on it or he talks himself out of it, you may be waiting for a very long time.

And like we talked about, most guys rarely approach.

And if you only have to pick from the men who approach you, you aren't getting to pick from the highest quality men, you're simply getting to pick from the most aggressive men in the room.

If you're willing to stick your neck out a little bit and invite men to come and approach you, you'll massively increase your odds of meeting and attracting the right type of man for you.

Find Out If He's Taken

You meet a guy and you start talking to him… now for the big question…

Is he single and available to date?

Some men will give hints to let you know, some men will try to find out whether you're single before they start trying to pursue you.

Some men will be married and won't tell you until you ask.

That's why you need to find out.

There's really only one really good way to find out if a guy is single or taken: you need to ask him directly.

But you should avoid anything that sounds like you're assuming that he's already taken… this usually just comes off sounding needy and desperate.

So instead, you should ask him this…

"Are you single?"

But when do you ask?

There's really only one good time to ask a guy this question and it's after he's deliberately hit on you in some way.

This could be as soon as he opens his mouth if he comes in very direct and shows a lot of interest.

It could be after a compliment. It could be after he makes a move.

The key is to wait until he's shown some type of romantic interest in you.

But you MUST ask a guy if he's single or not. Otherwise, you might end up falling in love with a married man, coming to me for advice about how to get him to divorce his wife...

And that's not a good place to be.

Get Him to Ask You Out

You may have already discovered that even if you feel like you had a great conversation with a guy, he may not ask you out or even get your number.

Why do you think this happens?

Assuming that he's single, it's for one of two reasons...

The first reason is that he's looking to gauge your interest. And if he thinks you don't have any romantic interest in him, he might end up in the "friend's zone," or there's a good chance you'll reject his advance, he may not pursue it.

Here are some ways that you can show him you that you want him to ask you out without coming on too strong.

The first way to do this is to **Plant the Idea in His Mind**.

What you want to do is get excited about something he does, something he likes, or some type of place that he talks about that he's gone before.

Sometimes guys will mention things to do to gauge a woman's interest because they're looking to take her out somewhere.

You can do this with anything but let's assume that he's talking about a movie that he wants to go see, you can say something like...

**"That move looks like it's so awesome, I'd LOVE
to go see it!"**

Or let's say that he mentions a hike that he likes to go on, you can say...

**"I've always wanted to hike that trail...
when do you usually go?"**

Or if he mentions a cool coffee shop or bar or something that he normally goes to, you can say...

**"Ooooo, that place sounds awesome! I've love to check it out
sometime."**

If he's got much social savvy, he should pick up on this.

There is a chance that he still won't get the message.

So you can go a lot more direct and still have it come across as attractive.

Here's something I call the **Specific Direct**.

This is when you actually suggest to him that he takes you out to something specific that you've been talking about together.

If you've been talking about hiking, you can say...

"You should take me out hiking sometime."

Or if you've been talking about a movie that's coming out, you can say...

**"You should take me to go see that movie
when it comes out."**

If you haven't had a conversation about somewhere that he might want to take you, the best way to bring something up that you might like is to use the phrase, "Have you ever...?"

Then once you talk about it for a minute, that's when you can tell him to take you there.

For instance...

"Have you ever been hiking on Green Mountain?"

Once you've talked about it say...

"You should take me there sometime."

The only catch about telling him that you should take him out to something specific is that he might get caught up in whether he wants to take you out to that specific thing or not.

If hiking to him is a way for him to get away from everything and he likes doing that alone, he might reject the idea of taking you there.

Or if he thinks that you might be a gold digger trying to get a free date night out of him before you disappear on him, he might reject the idea of taking you to something that costs money like dinner, movies, or drinks.

The gold digger struggle is real.

So, you can always open up the decision to him as to where he takes you. The best way to do this would be to say something that is what I call, **Generic Direct**.

You can say something like this...

"You should take me out sometime."

Again, it's simple and powerful. If he's attracted to you and single, this is a great way to show that you're interested in having him pursue something more with you.

The second reason that a guy won't ask you out is because he doesn't feel it enough for you or he thinks that you're not the type of woman that he wants.

The rest of this program is about how to make him feel like you're the type of woman he he's looking for.

22

Make Boring Conversations Fun

Getting to know someone can actually be really boring... haha!

After you've had conversation after conversation of the same topics over and over again, these topics can actually make a guy less attracted to you just because of how boring they are.

If you want him to feel like you're different than all the other women he's met, you'll need to communicate in a different way.

Doing this can also pull him out of his head and into the moment which will make him more connected to his emotions.

And the more you can connect him with positive emotions, the more he'll associate you with those emotions.

Basically, this can help you spark a connection with him and it can make the process of dating him and getting to know him a lot more fun for both of you.

All you have to do is use what I call the **Let Me Guess technique**.

You use this when you're discussing the "interview" questions like what jobs you have, where you grew up, and what you like to do for fun.

The way it works is this... you ask him one of these interview questions and then you immediately guess something that fun, silly, or just straight up ridiculous.

For instance, you might say something like this...

**"So, what do you do for work? Wait... let me guess...
you're a pole vault champion!"**

Another one for the job is this...

"Let me guess... you're an African Prince!"

Here's another fun one...

"Let me guess... I want to say either a spy... or a ninja!"

Then, whatever he says his job actually is, say...

"Well, I was close."

It's pretty ridiculous but it's also pretty funny.

Another interview question is the "What do you like to do?" question.

Let's say you're at a coffee shop, a fun way to phrase it would be this...

**"What do you like to do for fun... other than
flirting with me at a coffee shop."**

This is a variation on the Let Me Guess technique where you're also creating an assumption that he's flirting with you.

This is attractive and fun!

Another interview question is the "Where are you from?" question.

Here's another way that you could say that one and make it fun...

"Where are you from originally?... let me guess... China!"

Or here's another one...

"Let me guess... the future?"

Whatever you guess, it needs to be somewhere he's obviously not from. If he is from the future, make sure to get the future winning lottery ticket numbers and send them to me.

The key is just to make this fun and playful. Don't get too caught up in being serious and just enjoy your time with him.

The less pressure you put on figuring out if he's the one and the more you just enjoy yourself, the more he'll enjoy himself around you as well.

Commitment
Connection

PART 2

Make Him Fall In Love With You

Once you've met a guy, you've been having a conversation, and you're getting to know each other better, it's time to take things deeper with him.

If you want him to pursue you for a long-term committed relationship, he has to feel something for you at a deep emotional level.

He has to fall in love with you.

If he doesn't fall in love, he'll eventually just pull away from you because the desire to stay with you won't be strong enough.

He may even disappear altogether or "ghost" on you.

But if he does fall in love, he'll begin to push the relationship forward towards a commitment and a romantic relationship.

When a man falls in love, he'll start thinking about you all the time. You might start getting text messages from him, out of the blue, just checking in with you.

Commitment
Connection

He contacts you more often because thoughts of you are bouncing around in his head, swirling around his thoughts. And he won't be able to make it stop.

When he falls in love, he'll want to treat you like you're a priority to him in his life because you'll become a lot more important to him.

So how do you make a guy fall in love with you?

Here's the key...

You need to connect to his heart and build an emotional connection with him.

Initially, you need to get him excited about you.

Be playful. Be interesting. Be valuable.

You need to show him that you're valuable to yourself, to him, and to any man who would be lucky enough to be with you.

I'll show you how to connect with him in this way throughout this section.

Commitment Connection

The Love topics

The first few dates with a man are vital. You need to show him that there's more to you than just your looks.

You need to capture his heart and create a powerful emotional connection with him that shows him you're the right woman for him.

You need to make him feel like you're someone worth pursuing for a relationship, not just a casual fling.

You need to show him that you and your life are fun and interesting to the extent that he shifts his thinking to the idea that HE needs to convince YOU to commit to HIM.

That's what Love Topics are designed to help you do.

And you should talk about these things in the first few dates or times you meet with a guy to spark his interest and excitement about you.

If you don't, you run the risk of being a lot more into him than he is into you. You risk the dates being boring.

You risk not connecting with the man and having him feel like he needs to pull away or disappear on you.

Just to make this clear, let's first talk about some things that do NOT bring you closer to a man...

What Doesn't Bring You Closer Together

A big misconception is that commonalities will make you romantically closer to a man.

In truth, they work for creating and solidifying a friendship with him. You can have very few commonalities with a man and STILL become very close to him.

And you can also have a ton of commonalities with a man and have him disappear on you.

A good friend of mine actually recently broke up with a woman and he described her as someone who had more commonalities than anyone he's ever met, guy or gal.

He broke up with her because of a difference in values... which is much more important but we'll talk about that later on in this program.

The second topic that does NOT bring you closer to a guy is "guy topics."

I get women who come to me all the time in despair because they don't want to learn about football or politics.

But these do NOT bring you closer to a guy.

They might make you seem like a cool friend or a good drinking buddy... but they won't make you someone a man wants to romantically connect to.

The next way of talking to a man that doesn't work is something I call Masculine Behavior Topics.

These are things like swapping resumes with a guy, trying to "out-man" him or "one-up" him, or being incredibly sarcastic to a guy.

A lot of men do this to each other which is why I think some women do it with guys.

But it does NOT bring him closer to you. And it will almost certainly make most men feel like they can't trust being vulnerable around you because of fear of ridicule.

Best case scenario, you'll end up attracting a very feminine type of guy... which there's no problem with as long as you like those types of men.

Instead, you need to create intrigue and mystery, authentically connect to his masculine side with your feminine side, and get him excited about you.

How do you do it?

With the Love Topics, of course!

Topics That Make Him Feel Closer to You

The first love topic is something I call **Exciting Activities**.

Exciting Activities are fun things that you've either done in the past or that you're going to do in the future.

If you want to attract a man and keep a man, one of the most powerful ways to do that is to have an exciting lifestyle.

Have at least something interesting and remarkable that you do at least once a month.

A lot of women I talk to end up putting off living a fun life with the excuse that they're waiting for a fun man to come and be a part of it with them.

Don't do that.

You're much more likely to attract a fun or interesting man if you have a fun or interesting lifestyle.

If you tell him that you want to live an exciting life but you're sitting on the couch all day watching reruns, he's going to feel like you're not in alignment with the lifestyle that he wants to live, regardless of what you say.

So have fun things that you do once in awhile that you can bring up and talk about in a conversation.

The easiest way to bring stuff up like this is to use the phrase...

"Have you ever been...?"

For instance, if you went ice skating you can say...

"Have you ever been to the ice rink under the clock tower downtown? It's so beautiful there during Christmas!"

And it doesn't have to be anything too amazing. Even if you go on a walk once a week somewhere you can say...

"Have you ever been to Wash Park on a Sunday? It's so much fun there! I love just hanging out and watching people sometimes... in a non-creepy way of course."

The key is to have remarkable things that you've done and remarkable things that you're going to do.

And it doesn't even have to be things that you ACTUALLY are going to do. It can just be things that you WANT to go and do.

For instance, if you're thinking about going to a concert, you can say...

"Have you ever been to Red Rocks for a concert? I was thinking about going this weekend..."

This can lead into other fascinating conversations about things that you love to do or things that he loves to do.

The more you talk about fun and exciting things that you love and he loves, the more he'll start to feel excited about being around you.

You'll seem like an exciting or remarkable person. And the more he feels that way about you, the more of a positive emotional foundation you'll create for the future relationship that you'll have together.

The second love topic is **His Passions**.

I get women sometimes who complain that men don't talk much. If you talk to a man about his passions, he'll talk forever.

And this isn't necessarily his job either.

Some guys just work to live and have a job that supports whatever lifestyle they want to have.

Maybe their real passion is surfing, rock climbing, or volunteering... things that don't tend to pay very well.

An easy way to start this conversation is this...

> **"What gets you up in the morning?**
> **What do you really care about?"**

If he doesn't have anything that he's passionate about, that should be cause for concern for you, for a number of reasons.

But most men have passions, or at the very least, unfulfilled dreams.

And if you can get him to talk about them, it'll make him associate that passion or dream with you and it'll also make him feel like you're someone he can let his guard down around and really open up to.

A lot of people are used to getting judged for having passions, dreams, and interests. If you can show him that you're someone

he can open up to about this, he'll start to trust you to open himself up about other things as well.

So once he starts talking about his passion, just ask him questions about it. Get curious.

You don't need to know anything about the topic. You just need to get him to keep talking.

This can be very powerful.

The third Love Topic is something I call **Your Weird Little World**.

This is where he's going to get to know about you and who you are as a person.

Some women come to me and they think they need to act like a perfect person in order to attract a guy.

This isn't true.

Perfect is boring. Perfect isn't lovable. Perfection doesn't exist and everyone knows this.

And the more you pretend like you're perfect, the more people will wonder what's wrong with you.

Instead, you want to let him into your world and discover things about you.

Commitment
Connection

You'll want to talk about vulnerabilities that you have. But note that I'm not saying you should dump your baggage out for him to see.

Talk about vulnerabilities, especially in the initial stages of dating, need to be things that you've worked on the past that you've gotten over.

Here's a rule to follow: Don't talk about vulnerabilities if you're still bleeding from them.

If it's something that has hurt you, you'll need to have done some healing from it first.

Flaws that you have that you've worked on that show you're a real human being who is growing and figuring out the world like everyone else.

But it's the particular vulnerabilities that you have that make you unique, exciting, different and lovable.

What are some challenges that you've had in your life that you've been working on?

What are some unique, quirky things that you have in your personality or life that you can share with someone?

How can you be vulnerable about who you are without dumping all your baggage out onto a guy?

And if you don't know, baggage is stuff from your past that you haven't started working on yet.

So that guy that told you your boobs are too small in second grade and now you have insecurities about your breast size that you haven't gotten over...

That's baggage. Keep that to yourself for the time being. You can talk about that when you've already got him hooked.

But the fact that you used to be so scared of spiders that you would cry yourself to sleep at night but now you went to a pet shop and ran past the spider section without crying, that's a vulnerability you can talk about.

What makes you real and shows that you have a personality and depth to you?

The way to bring something like this up is by saying something like...

"Want to hear something crazy?
But you have to promise me you won't laugh..."

Or you can say something like this...

"Want to hear something really embarrassing?"

It can take a bit of courage to bring stuff like this up but it can do amazing things to bring you closer to a man you like.

Here's a quick example of what one of these stories might sound like…

"When I was younger, I went to school for journalism because I had dreams of changing the media for the betterment of the world. After I became I journalist I became so beaten down because journalists don't really get to change anything. So I got out of it and started working at a medical office because at least now I get to make a difference in someone's life."

You could obviously elaborate on this a lot but hopefully you get the idea.

Things don't always work out. We all have fears, insecurities and things that happen to us.

You can use these things from your life to connect on a deeper level with a man or you can try to hide them and pretend like they're flaws you have.

My suggestion is that you sit down and put together a list of things that have happened in your life that you can talk about that convey vulnerabilities that you've worked on overcoming and quirky things about your personality that you can convey.

The last Love Topic we're going to discuss is something I call **Value Stories**.

These are stories that convey things that are important to you and attractive parts of your personality.

Attractive qualities that you might want to convey are things like...

- Being nurturing or caring or taking care of someone
- Being a role model for someone younger than you
- Having passions or interests in your life
- Being fun or playful
- Being adventurous or spontaneous
- Being smart and/or curious about the world
- Looking out for important people in your life like friends and family
- Having a view and interest in the world that's larger than yourself

Again though, you'll want to convey values that are specifically important to you.

What qualities do you want to get across to a guy?

What stories do you have from your life that can convey those qualities and values?

This is a difficult one to give you exact words for without knowing you and your stories.

But you can put together some stuff fairly quickly if you put a little bit of time into thinking about it.

Tease Him Into Desire

If you want to get a man to desire you more, a fun and attractive way to do this is through teasing him.

Teasing can allow you to show interest in a man but also create a little mystery in a way that makes him want to pursue you.

It also shows him that he hasn't completely won you over yet and that you're interested but you're not convinced. And that's exactly what you want to convey to a man in the beginning stages of getting to know him.

It can actually be a lot of fun to do when you're already in a relationship as well as long as you do it in a playful and half-hearted way.

Teasing always has the undertones of a joke. It's supposed to be playful and funny.

The first type of tease we're going to talk about is saying something to show interest and then pulling it back a bit.

You can also do it showing disinterest and then showing interest after that.

This creates a space for him to come into and pursue you. And it's really attractive when used in moderation.

Here's an example of a good tease that can work pretty powerfully...

"You seem pretty awesome... so far at least."

You'll want to smile after you say that one to make sure he knows you're teasing him.

There has to be a bit of playfulness there when you do these, otherwise he might think you're being mean or cruel, which is not what you want to convey.

And you can definitely go too far with this stuff or use it too much, which is never a good thing.

But if you throw it in once in awhile, it can be incredibly charming, funny, and connect you to him emotionally.

Here are some other examples:

"You have a nice smile... but we need to
do something about those shoes!"

Or...

"You have a great smile."

And then when he says, "thanks," say...

"This is where you're supposed to compliment me back"

And then smile after you say that one...

Don't get too serious though. This is all about being playful and having fun and letting him know that you're being playful and having fun.

Flirt Like a Goddess

I meet some women who think that they should just lean back as far as possible and do nothing to figure out whether a guy is interested in them or not.

This is a bad strategy.

Most guys struggle for a decent portion of their lives to stay out of the "Friend Zone" with the women they want to date.

This is a very painful and agonizing position for men to be in and most dating advice that men look for is about how to stay out of the Friend Zone with women.

In fact, this was my biggest challenge when I first got into the dating industry as well. There's nothing more disheartening than being put into the Friend Zone by a woman that you've gone on dates with.

Most guys would rather have a woman "ghost them" or disappear completely than ever again hear…. "You seem really nice but I think we should just be friends."

Because of that, if a guy thinks that you MIGHT stick him in the Friend Zone, he may end up disappearing on you.

That's why you're better off flirting and showing some interest than leaning back completely and doing nothing, hoping for him

to continue pursuing a woman he might think isn't interested in him.

This also gives him permission to move things forward with you. Men are constantly looking for signs of permission that you want them to push things forward.

With flirting, just like with teasing, you'll want to keep it light, fun and playful.

The difference between flirting and teasing though is that teasing you're pulling back and creating a space whereas flirting is just showing interest in fun, playful ways.

It creates spikes in emotions when you do it with a guy and creates almost an addictive like feeling inside of him.

Sprinkle them into your conversations here and there and it'll be a lot of fun, you'll deepen his desire for you, and you'll encourage him to continue pursuing you.

The first one is something I call **The Mysterious Smile**.

All you need to do is look at him and start smiling...

When he says, "What are you smiling about?"

That's when you say...

> **"You don't want to know what I'm thinking."**

Then change the subject.

This will make him think that you're thinking something sexual about him... but you're not saying it.

And if he accuses you of thinking something sexual, say...

"Get your mind out of the gutter... you're totally into me."

Here's another one...

When he's talking to you interrupt him and say...

"Sorry, I'm a little distracted with how cute you are... say that last part again."

Telling a guy that he's cute is a good way to show him you're interested without coming on too strong.

After the first time a guy kisses you, say something like this...

"My daddy warned me about men like you..."

Another one is if you and a guy are obviously really into each other, you can say...

"It's too bad we don't like each other..."

And then crack a smile.

Flirting is really communicating interest in a very attractive way. You have to come from a space of confidence and playfulness or else it won't work.

Commitment Connection

It can't be about getting something from him, baiting him to compliment you, or quenching your insecurities... that will only come off as needy.

This stuff can be incredibly powerful if it's coming from a healthy place.

Here are some more...

If he hits on your or blatantly shows some interest in you, say...

"I bet you say that to all the girls..."

If a guy starts talking about how great he is or starts bragging about himself in some way, you can say...

"Really? That's not what I heard about you!"

Then laugh... you probably haven't heard anything about him and if he pries, just tell him that.

Another fun way to flirt is to flip the script on him and act like he's the woman and you're the guy...

For instance, if he asks you what you do, you can squint, look him in the eyes, get a little close to him like you're suspicious of him and say...

"You're not a gold digger, are you?"

Since guys are constantly worried about gold diggers (the struggle is real!), you can accuse HIM of being the gold digger and it can be pretty funny.

Another great thing to do is to wait for him to do things that you like…

For instance, if he pursues you, does gentleman things like opening doors, walking on the outside of the street, putting his jack around you…

If he does anything that you want him to do more of, reward him by saying things like…

"Wow, that was hot."

Or…

"That was really attractive."

As I've talked about before, it makes a man feel really good about himself when you show him sexual interest. And when you do it after he does something you like, it'll encourage him to do it more often.

Another way to flirt is just to show direct sexual interest, in an attractive way.

For instance, you might say…

"You look so sexy in that shirt"

Or…

"Your butt looks really good in those pants."

Remember:

This is all about having fun, being playful and showing interest. Don't dwell over any of these and don't take a joke too far or for too long.

If you get too caught up in jokes and being playful all the time, he'll begin to think it's an act and that's not attractive.

But sprinkling it throughout your interactions with a man is incredibly attractive and will spark and deepen his emotional and romantic interest in you.

Setting Irresistible Boundaries

If you haven't heard this before, you're hearing it now...

Men respect women who respect themselves. Men value women who value themselves.

That's why boundaries are important. Boundaries show that you value yourself and that you demand that the men you date treat you well.

But you're not doing it in a cold, angry, unattractive way. You're setting boundaries in a sweet, loving, warm way that's attractive to men.

You can also screen out men very quickly who try to walk all over you and won't respect you and treat you well.

Men tend to like to see how far they can push things with a woman. Many times, this isn't even conscious, it's just something we tend to do.

And it tends to bite us especially if we take things really far and then lose respect for the woman we were testing the limits on.

So it's important that you set strong boundaries and stick to them.

Here's how to set a boundary in an attractive way...

First you need to state what your desire is.

When you're setting your boundary, it's important to let that person know that you're still interested in them.

If you don't, he may get the wrong signal and think you don't like him anymore. This happens all the time. And if you don't want it to, make sure you reinforce your desire.

Second, say what the boundary is.

Make sure you say it in a clear, specific way so that he understands exactly what you're telling him and there's no room for interpretation.

Third, give the reason why you're setting the boundary.

A man is more likely to buy into whatever it is that you're saying if you give him a reason why this is your boundary. It's a psychological thing, just trust me on this one.

Fourth, ask him if he agrees to it.

For instance, let's say you want to get back early, you might say...

"I'd love to hang out all night but I need to get back before ten so that I can get some sleep before tomorrow. Can you have me back by 10?"

Here's another situation...

Let's say a guy calls you up in the middle of the night and wants you to come over for a booty call and you don't want to do the booty call thing.

Here's what you can say...

"That sounds like a lot of fun and I'd love to come over some night in the future. But I'd rather we meet up during the day for now so we can get to know each other a little better first. How about we meet up during the day this weekend?"

Now it is possible that he won't want to meet up with you on the weekend or even talk to you anymore after this... and if that's the case, that's fine because he wasn't looking for something serious with you anyway.

And as far as I'm concerned, I just saved you, weeks, months, or even years of being with a guy who is just going to look at you as a booty call.

I'd say that phrase was worth the whole value of this program!

Respect yourself and value yourself to only allow what it is that you want into your life.

He's either going to agree to your boundaries or he's not. And you're either going to stick to your boundaries or you won't.

My suggestion is that you do what you have to in order to stick to your boundaries so that any men you date or are in a relationship with will start to believe that you really are as valuable as you claim and will adhere to whatever boundaries you set.

Commitment Connection

PART 3

Make Him Feel Good

M en stay with women who make them feel good about themselves. If you want a man to stay with you, you need to become a source of his positive emotional experience.

The *Relationship Research Institute* found that couples who stay together experience 5 times as many positive emotions as negative ones in the relationship.

Researchers at the Institute can predict with over 90% accuracy whether or not a couple will stay together or break up.

As soon as one partner starts experiencing more negativity than the 5 to 1 ratio, the relationship is almost certainly doomed.

If you aren't in a committed relationship yet and you start to become a source of negative emotions for him...

For example, if you fight all the time when you're around each other...

If he feels like he can't talk to you about important topics...

If he feels like you're trying to change him, fix him, or get him to be different than he is...

If you're constantly pulling him away from his path and purpose in life...

If you're disrespectful towards him in public or in private...

He may decide that he's much better off being single than being in a relationship with you.

Many women take this to mean that men don't want relationships. But the truth is that men tend to take the idea of commitment very seriously.

But he doesn't want to commit to something that he's going to regret later on. He doesn't want to end up like his friend who are committed... many of whom might be stuck in relationships with no sex, with women who constantly attack them, and feeling like there's no way out.

Too many men have seen relationships that end up like this. So if you want him to stay with you, you need to become a source of positive emotional experiences for him, not negative ones.

In this section, we're going to discuss some of the best ways to make him feel good when he's around you so that you can keep him coming back forever.

Commitment Connection

Compliment Him

Everyone loves a compliment. If you don't like compliments, maybe you're not a human.

But human or alien, men love to get compliments because it makes them feel like they're doing a good job around you.

He's doing a good job and he's winning with you... that's what you want him to feel like.

There are different kinds of compliments that work with guys, here are some of them...

The Praise Compliment

Praise compliments are the most straight forward of all compliments. You're showing him that you admire him.

I have to warn you though...

Don't compliment a guy in order to get something from him, that's incredibly unattractive.

Don't compliment him to get him to respond to you in a certain way or to bait him into complimenting you back.

This signals neediness to a guy. And our natural inclination as people (women do this too) is to pull away from someone who is acting out of neediness.

Only compliment a man when it comes from a high value place. Use it as a gift to him, with no expectation of anything in return.

When you come from this place, it's incredibly attractive and a powerful way to bring you closer to a man.

Here are a few praise compliments...

"You're so smart."
"You look so great."
"You look so handsome."
"You are so cool."

Again, like I said, you need to come from a place of confidence and high value when you say these or they will make you seem needy or like you're trying to get something from him, which is not attractive.

What is attractive is getting a compliment from someone who is high value and confidence. Those types of people are the types of people we're dying to get compliments and validation from.

And what you're coming from that place, these can be incredibly powerful.

Think about it. Would you like to be told that you're beautiful, smart or cool by someone you like and admire?

Men do too.

Sexual Compliments

53

Men want to feel sexually desired by the women they're with. This makes them feel like a worthy man.

They want to feel like they can please your sexually. The best way for you to show a man that he's doing a good job with you sexually is to compliment him during sexual moments that you have together.

Here are a few simple ways to do this. You can say...

"You feel so incredible"

You can compliment his masculine presence by saying...

"You feel so strong."

Compliment his body by saying...

"I love the feel of your skin."

Or...

"I love the hair on your chest."

Complimenting the way he smells can be powerful too...

"I love the way you smell"

Don't underestimate the power of a good compliment to making a man associate good feelings and emotions to you.

This is incredibly important if you want to keep a man interested in you over the long-term of a relationship.

Compliment His Manliness

In an age when men and women both seem incredibly confused about what their roles are as man and woman, the guy you're seeing will want you to confirm to him that he's the man of the relationship, or at least he will be.

Men want to feel like they are men.

Not only does this make him feel good when he's around you, it also makes him feel like he can deserve the respect of other men in his life.

These can be really powerful, use them wisely!

The first one you can anytime he does something for you...

"Thanks for taking care of that for me."

Men want to feel like they're capable of being there for you. And when you say something like this to him, he'll feel like he's up for the challenge.

Here's one you can use when he's done something cool or significant, even if it has nothing to do with you...

"You're my hero."

Telling a man that he's your hero can make his heart melt. It's getting me teary eyed just thinking about it!

Here's one you can do any time he takes the lead on a date, spends time with you when you've been drinking, or takes care of something for you...

"I love that you know how to take such good care of me. It's really attractive."

This next one is something you can say anytime he's been acting like a guy at all. At first glance, this may not seem like it's attractive to a guy but guys like being told that they're guys.

Here it is...

"You're such a guy."

You'll want to say this with a smile and a head shake like you've caught him being a guy and it doesn't make any sense to you.

It can be funny, attractive, and a good ego booster for the guy.

Compliments Through Respect and Admiration

Most women I talk to want to be loved and cherished above almost everything else.

In the same way, most men want to be respected and admired above everything else.

It's something we learn very early in our lives, as children.

We fight on school grounds for admiration and respect. We fight in gangs for admiration and respect.

We go out and fight wars for admiration and respect. We marry women for respect.

And we work jobs we hate for respect.

If you can show him that he's earned your respect and that you believe in who he is, this can go a long way to making him feel like you're the perfect woman for him.

For instance, if you're talking to a man and he's having a hard time with something, you can say to him…

"I know you can figure it out."

Some of these are kind of deep and they're supposed to be. You're basically telling a guy that he's a powerful human being and you can see that in him.

And when you do that, it makes him feel like you're a part of his support system, which many guys have very little of in their lives.

Here's another one you can use when he's facing some type of challenge or talking about some type of goal that he's working on…

"I have faith in you."

Some women get stuck in the playful, flirty phase of meeting a guy and they don't really know how to transition out into something more serious and deeper.

These phrases are a good way to transition into that.

Here's the last one...

"I believe in you."

When you overtly tell a man that you believe in him, you need to make sure you know enough about him that you can say that and it doesn't make you look like you're just saying it to win him over.

We'll talk more about how to use this in a really powerful way to show a man that you're exactly the right woman for him later on in this program.

Accept a Compliment in an Attractive Way

There are two different types of compliments that men give to women. The first is a compliment to gauge her interest in him.

Usually this happens the first time you meet a guy. He might compliment you telling you that he thinks you're attractive.

The key here is not just to accept it well but to let him know that you're also attracted to him.

If you are attracted to him, you can say...

"Thank you... you're not so bad yourself."

If you're not attracted to him, just thank him for his compliment.

The second type of compliment is one that he gives you once you've been dating for a while or are in a relationship together.

The feminine role is the receiver.

And a woman who can receive well is very attractive to the masculine parts of a man and can show him that you're a good match for him.

PART 4

Make Him Commit to You

One of the biggest complaints that I get from women is that men don't want commitment. Men don't want to buy the cow when they can get the milk for free.

And don't get me wrong, I can definitely see how you might think that.

But thinking that men don't want commitment is far from the truth.

The truth is that most men do want commitment but we've become pretty bitter and jaded about the whole thing, with very good reason.

Men watch their friends, fathers, and hear stories about other men who have basically lost their manhood due to getting into committed relationships.

We hear about and know married men who haven't had sex with their wives in years (I have very close friends and family members who are in this situation).

Commitment
Connection

We hear about men losing half of their hard earned money to women who abuse and take advantage of them (Again, I have friends and family who have experienced this).

We hear about men not being able to hang out with their friends and their girlfriends and wives shaming them, belittling them, and forcing them to work hard for very little, if any, gratitude in exchange for it (More friends and family have experienced this).

As a society, if we're going to move towards having marriages that men want to get into and will last, this kind of culture needs to change.

This whole War of the Sexes thing that we have going on in America (most countries don't have this) is destroying our relationships.

You may have heard me mention this before but Gallup did a study of men aged 18 to 34 and found that 91% of them wanted to fall in love, get married, and have children.

91%!

And most men still want that when they get older... but the older we get and the more relationships we get into, the harder it is to keep that dream alive.

I know a lot of women who have given up that dream as well.

As a result, a lot of men have become a lot more cautious about who they get into relationships with and are even more cautious about the topic of marriage.

We don't want to end up like all these miserable men that we know.

But we still want companionship. We still want women who know us at a deeper level than anyone else in our lives.

We still want the support, nurturing and affection that comes from a relationship.

But it's like marriage changes people. And I know plenty of women who have said the same thing about men they married.

This section is about not only convincing a man that you're someone he can and should commit himself to...

It's also about building a foundation for a healthy, loving, secure relationship.

You have to convey a few things to a man...

You have to convey that you're on his side.

You have to convey that you're relationship and commitment material.

You have to convey that you're willing to allow him to choose you, instead of trying to force him and beat him into the commitment.

Men commit for their reasons, not yours.

And you also have to show him that this is something that you want and that you're not going to wait around forever.

Men commit because they feel something for a woman... they feel that it's "right" with her.

If he doesn't feel that it's right with you, he won't commit, and he'll have lots of good reasons not to commit.

In this section, I'm going to show you what you need to say in order to get a man to fell like you're the right woman for him to commit to.

Become Exclusive

One of the biggest mistakes a lot of women make is thinking that the way they date is the way everyone else dates as well.

I get women all the time who tell me that they only date one person at a time and they only want to meet others who date one person at a time as well.

It even goes so far that some of these women will only ever talk to one guy at a time. If they start a conversation with a man on a dating app, they ONLY talk to that one guy until things are resolved one way or another with him.

This is NOT how most people date. Most men and most women date multiple people at a time.

In fact, in our society right now, that's not only normal, it's expected.

So here's the deal...

If you don't talk with a man about whether he's seeing someone else or not, you can just assume that he's seeing other women until you do.

So if you want him to just see you and only you, you have to have some type of conversation with him about this.

The key to having a conversation like this with a man is to allow him to have the freedom of choice.

The more choice and freedom you give a man, the more he'll think that you're an amazing woman that he wants to give up his choice and freedom for.

I know this may seem contradictory but that's how it works.

He has to choose to be exclusive. If you try to force him into it, he'll do whatever he wants to do but he probably just won't tell you about it.

So how do you have this talk with a man?

It's kind of similar to setting a boundary with a man.

Here's how you do it...

1. *Say what you're doing.*
2. *Say the reason why you're doing what you're doing.*
3. *Ask him to inform you if he plans on doing or does something different.*

Let me give you an example:

"While I'm sleeping with someone, I don't sleep with anyone else. I just don't feel like there's any reason to sleep with someone else if I'm getting my needs met from one person.

I want to make sure you're doing the same. Will you let me know if you plan on or do sleep with someone else so I know where we stand?"

To a man, this feels like you're giving him the freedom to do whatever he wants... just so long as he's honest with you about it... instead of forcing him into something that he has no control or say over.

His answer to this will let you know where he stands with you. If he says anything other than "Yes"... as in if he says, "Sure..." then ask him if he's unsure about it.

And this doesn't have to be about sex... it could be about seeing other people in general or whatever aligns with your values in this area.

If you do it this way, you'll give him choice and make sure that you're getting what you want.

Regardless, I suggest you put exclusivity on the table either before you have sex with him the first time.

This will help you with your own personal wellbeing and will set the precedent of wanting to create a foundation for a healthy relationship.

If you let yourself get into a relationship where you're having sex, you don't know where things are going and things aren't going in the direction you want, there's a very high chance you're going to get into a situation you don't want to be in.

The Swan Technique

Being committed is more than just being exclusive with a man. Exclusivity is about limiting your sexual or romantic connections down to one person.

Commitment is about combining your lives together and having agreements about the type of relationship that you want to create, nurture and grow together.

It's setting the foundation for your relationship to grow in a direction that takes into account both of your needs and boundaries.

It's an expression of your love together that says that you want to create something that's more than just the two of you separate but is a third entity that brings both of you fulfillment, happiness, and meaning.

If he doesn't feel any need to be committed to you, you need to have a talk with him without freaking him out or making him feel bad about you or commitment.

It's possible that he's wanted to move things forward but wasn't sure exactly how you felt about it.

A lot of guys don't know when a woman wants a commitment... or if she wants one at all.

Commitment
Connection

Not all women want commitment. There's actually research done on this subject and what they found is that women leave relationships twice as much as men do.

Men just tend to be a lot more resistant to getting into the committed relationship than women are. But they tend to stay in it longer and through worse times.

If your man is the type of guy who has had women walk out on him before when he brought up the idea of commitment (it's happened to me), he may push the topic off even if he knows it's something you're interested in.

So how do you bring up this conversation with a man?

First thing you'll want to do is make sure it's good timing. Don't bring up serious conversations like this while he's in the middle of something.

Wait until he's relaxed and preferably has had some time to himself.

For men, this conversation can be incredibly challenging and emotionally draining.

The best way to start this conversation is to come from a place of gratitude.

Start off by saying something like this...

Commitment Connection

**"I really enjoy spending time with you and
I love how I feel around you."**

Second, come from a place of responsibility and desire.

It could sound something like this...

**"And I'm in a place where I'm ready to explore creating an even
better relationship together with you."**

*Third, let him know that there are some things you need to talk
about and checking in with him.*

It might sound like this...

**"Part of that is making sure we understand
each other fully. Sound good?"**

He'll probably be a bit curious and might be a little stand-offish if
he thinks that this is going to be about how he needs to change as
a person.

A lot of these conversations turn into a talk about how a man
isn't living up to expectations that a woman has.

Instead, I suggest that you come from a place of how you want to
contribute to the relationship or framing your needs as
something that you'd like to do.

And then once you've established a thing or two about stuff that
you want to contribute THEN you ask him if there's anything he'd
like to contribute.

And last, if there still any unresolved needs you have to communicate, this is the time to do it.

The reason you do it this way is that you're building up a contribution and commitment through your conversation.

And by the time you get to unfulfilled needs, it becomes a lot easier to bring them up when you've already contributed to the relationship.

Note: If he gets upset or triggered by something, that's an important thing to pay attention to.

What's he getting triggered by and is it legitimate?

A lot of times women will discount things that a guy says and explain it away as some kind of excuse or personalize it about themselves.

Sometimes women will make it mean that he doesn't love her enough or he'd just work it out and not have a problem there.

In my experience, that's rarely the case. Most likely, you should listen to what it is that he's saying and at least evaluate it at face value before you determine any deeper meaning to what he says.

You'll also want to look for any red flags in what he says. If he says that he doesn't want the relationship you're looking for or that he doesn't want it with you, those are red flags showing that he might legitimately not be in a place to be in that relationship with you.

That are other cases though, like if he says he's not ready. And we'll talk about that in the next section.

The important thing to do here, regardless of what he says is to avoid get defensive and going into any negative conflict patterns and instead embrace him and show him that you're on his team.

If you can effectively do that, especially against any criticism or concerns that he has, you'll come out of this in a very good spot.

He's Not Ready

Sometimes a man will say that he isn't ready for a relationship or the type of relationship that you're looking for.

Here's what this could mean...

- It's been a short period of time and he thinks you're trying to move things forward too quickly for him.
- He has insecurities that come up for him and he's worried that you'll find out the REAL him if he opens up and commits to you, and that scares him to death.
- He doesn't feel like he's ready to settle down yet and still has some exploring that he needs to do before he can get into a real relationship.
- He's been hit with something that takes up his time and he legitimately doesn't have time for the relationship you want (usually this involves his work).
- He believes that to be in a relationship, he has certain obligations to be able to provide for that relationship (usually from a monetary standpoint) and won't get into a relationship unless he can provide for it.

What it usually doesn't mean... it usually doesn't mean that he doesn't love you or that he doesn't want to be around you.

In most situations, when he says he's not ready, there's a way you can help move things forward with him and still get the relationship you want.

I've coached women through this process and a few of them have gone on to committed relationships and marriage.

Before we talk about what to do, I just want to make sure you know not to blame, condemn, or attack a man when this happens. You'll only make things worse and make him feel like he wants to fight back against you, which is not what you want.

If you want to see if things can move forward, here's what you need to do...

First, you need to ask him why he's not ready.

Don't leave this up to interpretation, let him tell you and take what he says at face value.

This simply sounds like...

"Why aren't you ready? What's stopping you?"

Second, you need to ask him what it will take for him to be ready.

It sounds simply like this...

"What will it take for you get through that and be ready?"

Third, you'll want to ask him how long it will take for him to be ready.

This might sound like this...

"How long do you think it'll take for you to get through this?"

Next, you'll want to determine whether what he says from the length of time is a period of time that you're willing to wait.

For instance, if he tells you that he needs to get his financial situation together. That could take 3 months or 5 years.

That's why you need to ask.

And if he tells you 6 months or longer, you have to determine whether that's a period of time you're willing to wait for.

If it isn't or he isn't sure about what he's doing or how long it will take or what he needs to do to get there, you, again, need to determine whether the man you're with is more important to you or having the relationship you want is.

You might end up waiting that time and he still isn't ready. That's why I suggest that you don't wait if it's going to take more than 6 months.

There's just no certainty there. You can do it if you want to but when you start getting to those numbers there's no real way to be certain of what will happen.

If he's not sure, my suggestion is that you create a boundary until he is sure.

That might go something like this...

"I really love you and enjoy being with you but I feel sad when I think I won't get into the relationship I want.

I really want to be with you but I also want a man who can step up and be with me so that we can create a beautiful relationship together.

I'm ready for that right now. So if you're not ready, this doesn't work for me anymore. I can't continue this with you."

Then you'll need to let him decide what he's going to do from there.

Hot/Cold On/Off Men

What if things kicked off really well with a man and then a pattern starts emerging…

Maybe he starts leaving and coming back to the relationship…

Maybe he starts going cold on you and then suddenly heating things up when you've almost completely given up on him…

Maybe he ignores you completely one minute and then smothers you with attention the next…

This is the Hot and Cold, On and Off again man.

It's a difficult place to be for you because it leaves you with so much uncertainty about him and the relationship that you may not really know what to do.

This could be happening for a variety of reasons…

It could have a lot to do with his work schedule. A lot of men have times in their work of high demand followed by times where they can relax and let go a little bit.

There may be other things that eat up his time here like kids from previous relationships or simply other commitments that he's made prior to you showing up in his life.

And while you may want to be his priority, the other things in his life end up coming before you.

Sometimes, it's just what's going on with a man.

Some men are just all over the place... sometimes they're up and sometimes they're down. And his presence with you is a reflection of how he's experiencing his own life.

It could be a reflection of his insecurities. It could be a reflection of patterns that constantly run throughout his life.

Regardless, the likelihood is that it has nothing to do with you and has everything to do with him.

The best thing to do is to first figure out what's going on with him. You need to figure out whether this is something that is just happening right now or if it's something that is a long-term pattern for him.

If it's something that's happening just right now, how long will it last. And more importantly, are you willing to wait for it to stop.

The best way to find this out is to have a conversation with him.

Here's how you might want to start it...

"So I'm feeling a little frustrated and I was wondering if you could help me with something. Is this a good time to talk?"

If he says that it is a good time to talk, say this to him...

"I really enjoy the time we have together but it seems like you've been really busy lately. Do you have something going on?"

And if he says that it's something that's just started, ask him this...

"How much longer do you think this will last?"

When he tells you, you need to figure out if his time phrase is something that works for you. Don't be a victim to his lifestyle.

If it doesn't work for you but it's something that's pretty ingrained in his life, you need to make a decision as to whether having this man or having the relationship you want is more important.

If this is a long-term pattern, there's probably not much you'll be able to do to fix the pattern for him. He may be in it for the rest of his life.

You can always try giving him a chance though. Although, these usually look like ultimatums and ultimatums usually don't work out.

Not because there's anything wrong with an ultimatum but because the person's behavior is so ingrained that there's not much you can do to change it.

And if you're serious about the ultimatum, there's a good chance the person could pick either one.

If it isn't a long-term pattern and it is something that's only here for a short period of time, you need to decide whether you're willing to wait that time.

If you do decide to wait, you should slow things down with him when he comes back to you. And you may even want to distance yourself and meet other men.

You don't want to be stuck waiting for a man who may or may not get it together enough to be with you in the near future.

Regardless of what it is, here's something you can say with him...

"I really enjoy being with you but I want to be with a man who can make me a priority in his life and consistently be around. If that's not you, I need to know so I can move on and find a partner who can be here with me."

Commitment
Connection

Keep Him From Pulling Away

When you're in a relationship with most men, they'll want to get closer to you. This may seem like it's not the case, especially if your man is pulling away.

But pulling away is a normal and natural thing that a lot of guys do in a relationship. And many times, it's the women who are the ones who pull away and need space, so don't think it's just men.

Also note that this is different from the hot/cold man because of the amount of time. Hot/cold men usually are cold for much longer periods of time before they come back and they doing it frequently and regularly.

When I talk about a man pulling away, I'm talking about him doing it for short periods of time, every once in awhile.

The main reason this happens in relationships is because a guy needs to process his emotions.

There are other possible reasons like he might have a lot going on at work or problems with his kids or something like that.

But the main reason is that he needs to process things.

This may seem alien to a lot of women especially if a guy pulls away after getting close when it seems to fill you up and make you want to continue to get closer.

Here's what you need to do when a guy pulls away...

Leave him be and give him some space. Lean back and let him process and go through whatever he needs to go through.

The overwhelming majority of times, things are okay with the two of you if he's pulling back, especially if you had just gotten close.

I know the most frustrating part might be to have faith that things are okay with him but that's the challenge you need to make for yourself.

Reframe what's going on and what's in your head to have faith that he still loves you and everything is okay.

If you attempt to move towards him when he pulls away like this, you're probably going to make things worse instead of better.

When he's away from you, he'll build you up in his mind. But if you're bugging him and trying to connect when he needs time away, that can quickly change.

Remember: Give him space and he'll appreciate you for it.

Have things that you can do that you can occupy your mind and time with so that you're not obsessively thinking about him.

How to Make Him Not Want to Pull Away

One of the mistakes that a lot of women make is condemning or shaming a man who pulls away from them.

He comes back from pulling away into his cave and she'll attack him and tell him he's inconsiderate and bad.

This is the exact opposite of what you want to do. If you attack a man when he comes back, you're just creating a situation where you're punishing him for coming back to you.

Instead, you'll want to show him some gratitude when he comes back.

When you first hear from him, if you say...

"It feels so good to hear your voice!"

He'll feel rewarded and like it's safe to come back to you.

And if you treat him well when he does come back, you'll end up making him want to come back faster instead of staying away for so long.

Make sure you say things like...

"It's so good to see you again!"

And if you can make him feel safe enough around you and like you won't create more emotional intensity for him, he may even want to bring you around when he's in the state that he feels like he needs to get away from things.

The Life Partner Script

There are a lot of things that are different about men and women...

Men tend to be less emotional and more logical (at least we like to think we are)...

Men tend to be single focused where women are better at things like multi-tasking...

But MOST of the things we ultimately want are the same....

We both want to be loved and cared for...

We both want someone who accepts us fully for who we are...

We both want a life-partner, or a companion who knows us and understands us better than anyone else in the world.

That's why if you want a man to look at you like you're his companion, his life partner, you have to show him that you understand him as least as well as anyone else does.

Fortunately, most people are so wrapped up in themselves that connecting with a man in this way is something you're definitely capable of.

If you're ready to show a man that you really understand him in a way that makes him feel like you're that life partner to him, then you need to use what I call **The Life Partner Script**.

This is powerful and effective and will make him feel very close to you.

Here's what you need to do.

First, you need to figure out what it is that he's passionate about.

He may not be passionate about his career. And if he's not, that's fine. A lot of times, men are in careers because they need to make money and it isn't what they really care about most.

I have a friend who is very passionate about rock climbing. He doesn't make rock climbing his career but he loves it and likes to spend a lot of time doing it.

It allows him to fulfill his sense of adventure, be out in nature, and tackle tough challenges.

I have another friend who loves music and wants to become a really good musician.

He doesn't make money doing it but that's what he's really passionate about in his life.

If your man isn't doing something as a career that he really loves, here are a few questions you can use to discover what he's really passionate about:

"If time and money weren't an issue, what would you do with yourself?"

These questions are about getting him to dream. Many of us have forgotten our dreams.

Some of us have been told that we shouldn't dream, that it's not okay to.

What you're doing here is getting him in touch with powerful emotions that drive his dreams and motivations in life.

Here's another one you can use...

"If you had the complete support of the people around you in your life, what would you change?"

You'll want to use one of these that really resonates with you.

Or if you're having a hard time getting him to open up and talk, you could use more than one of these questions with him during the course of one or more conversations.

Here's another one...

"If you knew you weren't going to fail, where would you go or what would you create?"

Another thing that you'll want to do is probably write down your answer to these questions.

When you ask stuff like this, it's possible he might start asking you the same thing.

And if you know the answers, it'll connect him more to you and show him that you have depth of character, which will make him feel closer to you.

Here's the last one...

"Well, what did the five year old Dustin (or whatever his name is) want to be when he grew up?"

Based on whichever one of these questions you ask him, you should have a good understanding of what he's passionate about or who he wants to become.

Second, look for traits in him that show that he can do the things he wants to do or become the person he wants to become.

What you're going to show him here is that you really believe in him. And the way to do that is to find behaviors, personality traits or something about him that proves that he can do it.

For instance, let's say that he really wants to own his own business...

You could take any number of different personality traits and link them to how you could see him being successful owning a business.

Maybe he's caring... maybe he's driven... maybe he's hard working or is good with people or has good ideas or is good with numbers.

Any one of those things (and many others) could be linked to why you could see him as being a successful business person.

Third, get excited with him about his vision and share with him that you can see him achieving it.

This can be incredibly powerful so prepare yourself for that.

When you reflect this back to him, he may end up using it as fuel towards pursuing and becoming the man who he wants to be in his life.

That's why this connects a man so much with you. This can drive his passion to become the man he wants to be.

Very few people have someone in their lives who really believes in them. That's another reason why this is so powerful.

Most people simply connect on commonalities or superficial aspects of their lives. What you're doing is getting into the core of who he wants to become and reflecting the possibility back to him.

This is something that most men wish they had on a regular basis. And many have never experienced someone who has said this kind of stuff to them before.

You may have a leg up on connecting with him more than anyone else he knows, including his family.

For this to work, you have to be genuine, sincere, and authentic in your communications with him.

If he feels like you're just saying this to him without sincerity, he won't believe you and this won't connect with him.

Because of that, you don't want to say anything generic or that seems like you're just saying it to say it. What you say must really tie into who this person wants to become.

And the more detailed it is, the more likely it is to connect with him. If what you say can be applied to any guy, it probably won't work.

Fourth, break the tension by teasing him or flirting with him.

There'll probably be some tension in the air when you get done saying this to him because it'll get pretty serious.

You'll want to break that tension and push the mood towards something more playful and less serious so that you can go back to a normal conversation.

So this is what the process looks like in its entirety:

1. **Figure out what he's passionate about or who he wants to become.**

2. **Look for traits in him that show he can do the things he wants to do or become the man he wants to become.**

3. **Get excited with him about his vision and share with him that you can see him achieving it.**

4. **Break the tension by teasing him or flirting with him.**

For instance, let's say that you find out that he wants to become a really good salesperson. And you figure out that he's really attentive and seems genuinely interested in you. This is something that you could say:

> **"I can tell from the way you ask me questions that you have a genuine interest in people. And you have a very kind and loving heart. I can't really say that about a lot of people I meet. I think you're going to become an amazing salesperson. And I mean that... I'm not just saying it to get in your pants. :)"**

When you tease a guy, it should always be done in a playful tone. If you say something and it comes off as if you don't like him, it would come off as really strange instead of light hearted and fun.

Also, you can use a sexual undertone to the flirty comment. As we've talked about, guys want to be sexually validated by women.

What this means is that they want to know that you feel you get turned on by them, even if you're not ready to do anything with him sexually yet.

It's like metaphorically dangling a carrot in front of him. As you may know, men love sex.

And if you're in a situation where you haven't had sex yet, the last thing he wants is another woman who he's romantically interested in that only sees him as a friend.

But even if you have had sex before, the flirty comment still works.

Here are some ways that you playful flirting things to say after you reflect back traits that he has shown which tell you he could become who he wants to be:

**"I mean that... I'm not just saying it because
I think you're hot."**

"I mean that... I'm not saying it just to get in your pants."

"I mean that... I'm not just hitting on you."

Here are some teasing comments that you could use to break the tension:

"Too bad you're such a dork."
"Now we need to do something about those shoes."
"Now we just need to work on matching your clothes."

Commitment Connection

The Life Partner Script is all about showing him that you accept, understand and support him. It's about showing him that you believe in him.

If you can show him that you really get and understand him in this way, he'll decide that you're the perfect woman for him.

PART 5

Other Make Or Break Moments

The Enlightened Expression Technique

There's a myth out there that men think that emotions and emotional expression is drama.

This is ONLY true if that emotion comes along with expectations. We'll talk more about that in a bit.

If you do it the right way, expressing your emotions to a man can actually pull him out of his head and into his heart.

It can make him feel more connected to his emotions which will then make him feel more connected to you.

But this isn't all about him, of course.

The big reason this is important is because it allows you to finally express yourself in a way that's attractive, instead it being unattractive.

It will give you permission to feel and express your feelings around a man and men altogether.

If you've had problems expressing yourself around men, I don't need to tell you how important this is, you already know.

So let's start off with talking about what NOT to do...

Do NOT criticize him, condemn him, blame him, or create expectations around what he should say or do when you use this technique.

If you do that, you'll end up just pushing him away and creating a space that isn't safe for you to express yourself...

And it'll make him feel like you don't love and accept him for who he is...

Which basically turns into a spiral of bad things that you don't want to happen.

How to Have the Conversation

There are really two different instances that we'll talk about here.

The first one is when you need to have a real conversation with him about important feelings that have come up for you.

The reason this is an important distinction is that having an important conversation like this needs to be done at the right time...

Otherwise you risk overloading your man's brain, which will cause him to short circuit and need repairs before he starts working again.

Here's how you ask him whether it's a good time or not...

93

"Something has been bothering me. It's about money. I feel like I need to express myself. Is now a good time?"

This lets him know that you want to talk and that it's serious...

Obviously, that particular one is about money but it could really be about anything.

Here's another one that plays on his feelings of wanting to be your hero and help you out...

"I'm feeling really bad. Can we talk? I need your help..."

They key is to try using both of these and seeing how he reacts to them.

Some guys will react more favorably to one than the other, so test them out but they both work to set things up.

If it's a serious conversation that you need to have, make sure you ask if it's a good time because it could make a big difference in how he feels about the conversation.

The second instance is when you don't have a serious conversation to bring up, you're just expressing how you feel.

Fortunately, there's no setup necessary for this second instance.

How to Express Yourself in an Attractive Way

So let's talk about actually expressing yourself...

This is the most important part and where most women end up pushing a guy away.

Here's what you need to do...

First, when you express yourself, start by saying "I feel" or "I'm feeling."

What a lot of women do is they'll start off blaming, criticizing or even baiting a guy.

These are all toxic behaviors and will lead to a toxic relationship and the man feeling bad about himself and about you.

Instead, if you come from a place of expressing exactly what you feel, it's a lot more neutral and powerful. The guy doesn't feel pressured and he doesn't pull back.

If you normally blame, criticize, condemn, bait or do something else, it might take a few times of doing this for your man to relax around you when you do it.

Second, you'll want to state how you feel without making it about him or what he's doing.

I can't emphasize this enough... if you want to express how you feel, just express how you feel.

Don't make it about him or what he's doing.

Here's an example of what NOT to say...

"I feel like you've been such a jerk lately!"

Or this...

"I'm feeling like you just don't care about me
and our relationship!"

Those statements make it all about him.

You want to do the opposite, make it about what's going on with you and how you're feeling.

Here are some examples...

**"I feel really sad right now. I just feel like I'm alone and don't
have any support."**

Or this one...

**"I'm feeling overwhelmed and like
I'm not ready for this yet."**

Or another...

"I feel really nervous about where this is going."

Here's more...

"I feel like I'm having such a great time!"

"I'm feeling a little silly right now."

**"I feel very uncomfortable when I see money being spent so
quickly. Here's what I was thinking..."**

Notice that none of it is about him. It's all about you and how you feel.

As soon as you turn it into being about him, things start falling apart. So instead, just make it about you and how you feel.

Third, let whatever happens happen. Don't be invested in the outcome.

I know this can be really hard if you want something to happen based on what you've expressed.

But you have to let go of the outcome. You don't have control over it.

And there are much better ways and much better times to try to get him to do what you want him to do.

If you want to express how you feel, make it about expressing how you feel.

And allow a different time to be about getting him to do what you want him to do.

If you have something strategic that you need to talk about, like with the money one where you need to talk about something involving how your money is spent together in the relationship, make your expression of how you feel and the conversation about what you think the two of you should do as separate.

You conclude talking about how you feel and you start talking about what you think should be done. Don't mix them together or it won't turn out well.

So that's it.

Here are the steps again...

1. **If you need to have a serious conversation about something, start by asking him if it's a good time to talk.**

2. **When you need to express how you feel start by using "I feel" or "I'm feeling."**

3. **State how you feel without making it about him or what he's doing.**

4. **Don't be invested in the outcome.**

Get Him to Do What You Want Him to Do

Most people want their partners to start doing something a little different...

Most women want men to fix men...

Most men want their women to stop trying to fix them...

That was a joke but there's a lot of truth to that.

Here's the truth...

Men want to make women happy. And if you're not happy, a man's going to get stressed out and feel pressured.

Most men will bend over backwards to do things for the woman in their lives.

And you may think that men just know what you think they should be doing... they don't.

If you want him to be more loving and affectionate, you need to let him know how to... in a way that makes him want to without turning him off, making him feel bad about himself and you, wanting to hide things from you, or creating unnecessary conflict.

That's why you should use something called...

Instructive Appreciation.

Instructive Appreciation is when you appreciate him in an instructive way (very descriptive, I know).

You appreciate him for something WHILE you're telling him what you want him to do.

It's very smooth and ninja like and guys LOVE it.

You may have noticed a running theme throughout this program...

Condemning, baiting, criticizing, manipulating, forcing, nagging, kicking and screaming, crying and stomping your feet... these are all things that don't work.

They might get you attention.

They might get him to do something momentarily.

But they ALWAYS backfire in the end.

Why?

Because a guy doesn't want to be bossed around (some more feminine guys like it but masculine guys don't).

Guys don't want to be looked down on. They don't want to feel like they have to fight the woman in their lives.

They don't want to feel like you want them to change.

They want to be accepted and loved for who they are, just like you hopefully do.

First, let's talk about what doesn't work…

What doesn't work is saying sound vague statement and hoping that he gets the hint.

Here's an example…

"It's cold out here."

Now, it's possible he might think to himself, "Hmm… she's cold, I should warm her up."

But it's also possible that he might think, "She's right, it is cold, I should make sure my jacket is zipped up."

There's a good chance he has NO idea what you want him to do.

Instead, if you want him to warm you up and put his arms around you, using Instructive Appreciation, you can say…

"I love it when you put your arm around me."

This will make him want to put his arms around you.

Here's another example of something that probably won't work and almost certainly won't work in the long run…

"Why don't you hug me more often?!?"

But using Instructive Appreciation, you can get him to lovingly hug you by saying…

"I love it when you hug me. It's such a turn on."

He'll be hugging you every chance he can get with that one for many of the reasons we've been talking about early in this program… sexual validation, appreciation, instructive…

What doesn't work is starting sentences with "Why," like…

> **"Why didn't you cuddle me last night?**
> **Don't you love me anymore?!?"**

What does work is Instructive Appreciation where you might say…

"You know what would really turn me on? If you just held me in your arms for 5 minutes before we went to sleep at night. That would mean so much to me."

I hope you're getting the gist here. Instructive Appreciation is really powerful and there's a much better chance that it will get you what you want.

Just to let you know… sometimes you may have to give him this Instructive Appreciation more than once so that he'll remember what it is that you said.

Repetition is the mother of getting him to do what you want him to do and making him feel good at the same time.

Here are some more…

"You seem like the type of man who knows how to really take
charge of a situation. I really
admire that. It's very sexy."

Or...

"I love it when you buy me little gifts!"

Or...

"It means so much to me when you tell me
how beautiful I look!"

Instructive Appreciation is the way to get a guy to do what you want him to do without turning him off or pushing him away.

It works so try it out.

Commitment
Connection

Connect With Him

Sometimes, you may feel like you need to connect with your man.

And all too often, both men and women perceive each other's connection attempts as attacks or attempts to change the other person.

It's very important that when you feel like you need to connect with him, you don't accidentally push him away or make him feel threatened in some way.

So let's talk again about what works and what doesn't.

What doesn't work... again if you forgot from the last few chapters...

What doesn't work is condemning, blaming, baiting, attacking, etc.

What does work is this...

Compassionate Conversation.

Almost everyone I talk to realizes to some extent or another that being compassionate is valuable in a relationship.

Personally, I think this is the most important things that you can add to your tool chest of techniques to connect with a man,

eliminate conflict, and make a man feel like you're the most amazing woman in the world.

But since we're specifically talking about connecting with a man, let's talk about that.

Let's say you're trying to figure out how a man feels.

Here's what doesn't work...

"You never tell me how you feel!"

Instead, having a Compassionate Conversation may sound something like this...

"Lately it seems like there's been some kind of wall between us. I want to make sure that you're doing well. Are you okay?"

You're going from basically attacking his behavior to being a loving partner who wants to make sure he's okay.

Or maybe you're in a situation where you feel like he's becoming distant and checked out and you want to connect with him.

Here's what doesn't work...

"Why do you always pull away from me?"

Having a Compassionate Conversation sounds something like this...

"I'd like to be closer to you right now but I feel like you're having trouble with something."

There's something that you need to know though, so that you don't get yourself into any trouble.

Most men need space sometimes. And if he's going through a lot and his way of dealing with things is to pull away and get some space, you're better off giving him space and connecting with someone else, like a friend or family member.

When you're in relationship with a man, there are certain times when you need to place faith in the relationship and the fact that he still loves you.

Knowing that compassion is important and being compassionate are two completely different things.

If you want a man to truly value you as a companion and a partner, you need to have compassion for him and his situation, come from a space of compassion when you talk to him, and give him space if he needs it.

You're much more likely to get more of the connection you want if you do it that way.

The Goddess formula

I have a 3 part formula that I call The Goddess Formula.

This formula is the fastest and most effective way to be irresistible to the man you want.

When I coach a woman and talk to her about what's going on and the challenges she's having with her attracting the relationship she wants, it almost always boils down to one of these three things being out of alignment.

First, I want you to imagine that you meet a guy for a first time...

Tell me, which would you be more attracted to:

a. A guy who has no idea how to talk to you, what to say, and says a bunch of dumb things and makes meeting you awkward... or...

b. A guy who knows how to talk to you, makes you feel good about yourself and him, and maybe even turns you on a little bit?

I can already tell you that for the majority of women, the answer is b.

And for a man, it's really the same thing...

That's why the first part of The Goddess Formula is...

Communication.

As you know from owning this program, one of the most important aspects to attracting the man you want into the relationship you want is how you communicate with him.

Communication is all about what you say, the body language you use, and how you dress and present yourself.

It's ALL aspects of communication that you have with a man.

And communication is the best way to get you into the relationship you want…

But the other two aspects of The Goddess Formula keep him there.

So I want you to imagine that you meet this guy and he says all the right things, but then you start to notice something with your intuition…

There's something about him that you can just tell that he doesn't like women very much…

He thinks they're the problem and the reason why good relationships don't exist anymore.

If you knew that he felt that way, how would that make you feel?

If you had any self-respect, you wouldn't want to date a guy who dislikes women.

And the same applies for men… if you think men are the problem…

If you think men are all liars and cheaters…

If you think there aren't any good men left out there, that they don't want a real woman, a man is going to pick up on that and immediately place you in the category of "Not Relationship Material."

That's why the second part of The Goddess Formula is your…

Beliefs.

When I was in college, I was a part of a bunch of different research studies, just as a normal part of the student experience there.

One day we had a bunch of researchers come into our classroom with different colors of Kool-aid and they put the Kool-aid into little cups and we had to drink them and try to guess what flavor each color was.

And naturally, most people who drank the orange thought it was orange, they thought purple was grape, red was cherry, and so on.

Well, it turned out that ALL of the different colors were ALL apple, with different food coloring in each of them.

So why did everyone think that the different colors were different flavors?

Because if we perceive something to be true, we'll experience it that way regardless of whether that's actually how it is or not.

So if you believe that ALL men are liars and cheaters, even if you meet the perfect man for you, you'll find evidence that isn't even there that he's a liar and a cheater.

That's why it's so important to make sure that your inner world, your beliefs and thoughts, are in alignment with attracting the man and the relationship you want.

But think about this...

Imagine you meet this guy. You hang out and he seems awesome.

He says the right things, he does the right things, then you ask him a little bit about himself...

He says that he has nothing else going on in his life and he's just been sitting around waiting for you to show up.

He obsessively contacts you and asks you what you're doing and where you're going and who you're doing it with.

That's because he's missing the third component of The Goddess Formula, which is...

Lifestyle.

I get women who come to me all the time and when I ask about their lifestyle, they tell me that they're waiting for a man to show up in their lives before they really start living it.

I have some news for you, a man will be much more attracted to you if he thinks you ALREADY have an interesting life that HE wants to come and be a part of than if you're sitting around waiting for a man to show up to start it.

And a lot of times, what happens, is a woman will end up losing herself completely to the relationship because she gives herself completely to it.

And while this may seem noble, it's incredibly unattractive to a man.

What's a lot more attractive is having your own life outside of a relationship that you're in.

Have your own passions. Have your own friends. Have things that you can go and do outside of the relationship.

And have them separate from the relationship.

That way if a man pulls away, you're not obsessively thinking about him, texting and calling him, and trying to latch onto him.

You can give him space before he needs it, which is incredibly attractive to most guys.

So that's the three components of The Goddess Formula. Again, they are...

1. **Communication**

2. **Beliefs**

3. **Lifestyle**

Every woman that I've ever coached, when she had a problem attracting a man or getting him to move things forward towards having the relationship she wanted, it always boiled down to one of the three things in The Goddess Formula.

If you're interested in learning more about how to develop the beliefs or lifestyle components that you need to have the relationship you want, make sure you visit my website and look at the other programs I offer.

The Secret to Attracting a Man Who Loves You, Sees You, And Cherishes You Into A Committed, Lasting Relationship...

You want to be loved and cherished by a man. You want a man who feels like you're too important to him to lose you.

But we live in the age of the "hookup culture" where casual, friend with benefits situationships have become the norm.

Maybe you get into a situation where you give your everything only to be taken for granted, have the guy pull away, and eventually disappear on your altogether.

This makes you feel confused, frustrated, and feeling like you doubt yourself and your own worth... wondering if you'll ever get into the relationship you want.

If you're having a hard time with men and dating, it's not your fault. We live in a culture that encourages superficial relationships and discourages anything meaningful.

I believe there's a better way for men and women to get into and stay in committed relationships that last. That's why I put together a proven path that will help you get into the relationship you want.

It's called, "The Forever Woman."

Since 2005, I've taught, coached, and spoken to hundreds of thousands of both men and women, all over the world, about dating and relationships. My videos and articles reach millions of women, every month, all over the world.

Many of them have gone on to get married, raise families, and live happily ever after. I've helped save marriages, mend broken hearts, and heal struggling relationships.

And now I'd like to help you get into the relationship that you want using the formula that's helped many of my client's.

Your Success Path

I have a 3 part plan for you to be successful...

1. *Believe in your value*
2. *Position yourself in value*
3. *Communicate your value*

Go to TheForeverWomanFormula.com, watch the video on the page, and sign up for my free course, The Forever Woman Program.

If you get The Forever Woman and use the principles in it...

- You'll attract a man who loves and cherishes you
- He'll pursue you for a committed, lasting relationship
- You'll do less work and feel more appreciated and valued by your man.

If you don't get it...

- You'll stay stuck in your problems and challenges with men.
- You'll feel like you're doing everything in a relationship only to be taken for granted, have guys pull away, and eventually disappear on you
- You'll wonder if you're ever going to get into the relationship you want.

Go to TheForeverWomanFormula.com and check it out for free... if you decide you want to stay a part of our community, you can learn about how to do that as well there.

Talk soon,

Matthew Coast
CommitmentConnection.com

Printed in Great Britain
by Amazon